X

hockey's
new wave

Scott
Gomez

Open Up the Ice

BY
MARK STEWART

THE MILLBROOK PRESS
BROOKFIELD, CONNECTICUT

M

THE MILLBROOK PRESS

Produced by
BITTERSWEET PUBLISHING
John Sammis, President
and
TEAM STEWART, INC.
RESEARCHED AND EDITED BY MIKE KENNEDY

Series Design and Electronic Page Makeup by
JAFFE ENTERPRISES
Ron Jaffe

All photos courtesy AP/ Wide World Photos, Inc., except the following:
SportsChrome USA: Greg Forwerck, photographer — Cover
Anchorage Daily News — Pages 9, 12, 14, 17, 44
The following images are from the collection of Team Stewart:
The Upper Deck Company (© 1992) — Page 25
The Hockey News (© 2000) — Page 32
Fleer Corp. (© 1993) — Page 40
Sports Illustrated for Kids (© 2000) — Page 45

Printed in the United States of America

Published by
The Millbrook Press, Inc.
2 Old New Milford Road
Brookfield, Connecticut   06804

www.millbrookpress.com

Library of Congress Cataloging-in-Publication Data

Stewart, Mark.
    Scott Gomez : open up the ice / by Mark Stewart.
        p. cm. — (Hockey's new wave)
    Includes index.
    ISBN 0-7613-2268-X (lib. bdg.)
    Gomez, Scott, 1979– Juvenile literature. 2. Hockey players—United States—Bibliography—
Juvenile literature. 3. Hispanic American hockey players—United States—Biography—Juvenile
literature. I. Title. II. Series.
GV848.5.G66 S74 2001
796.962'092—dc21
[B]
                                                                                              2001030291

1 3 5 7 9 10 8 6 4 2

Contents

Playing Small, Dreaming Big

"I call him a freak of nature."

— CARLOS GOMEZ

More than a quarter of a million people live in the city of Anchorage, Alaska. Most families have an interesting story about how they got there. One of the strangest belongs to Scott Gomez, whose parents, Carlos and Dalia, met and married in Alaska in 1976.

Carlos was the son of migrant farmworkers, who would travel north from their home in Mexico to pick fruits and vegetables in California. This was a very hard life. His family was very poor and did not have access to hospitals or decent schools. Once one of Carlos's brothers had a broken arm. Because he did not receive proper medical care, the arm became infected and had to be amputated.

When Carlos was old enough for school, his father sent him to live with an aunt in the city of San Diego. Carlos had been born in the California town of Modesto, so by

How Scott Gomez went from Alaska to the NHL is one of the great stories in hockey. How his family came to live in Anchorage is one of the most incredible.

"I hated hockey. I wanted to quit."

SCOTT GOMEZ

law he was a United States citizen. That meant he could legally live in the United States and get a good education. It was a hard choice for Carlos's father to send his son away, but it was for his own good. Sadly, Carlos never saw his father again.

After Carlos graduated from high school, he heard about job opportunities in Alaska, where a long fuel pipeline was being constructed. The work was hard and the weather was cold, but the pay was good. In 1972 he got a job on the pipeline as an ironworker. Four years later, Carlos met Dalia. She had been born in the city of Medellín, in the South American country of Colombia. At the age of five she was taken by her father (against her mother's wishes) and brought to live with relatives in Brooklyn, New York. A year after that she moved with her father to Alaska, where it would be impossible for her mother to track her down. Dalia was attending high school in Anchorage when she met Carlos in 1976.

A few years after they married, Carlos and Dalia had two children. Monica was born in January of 1979, and Scott was born the same year, just two days before Christmas. The Gomezes had another daughter, Natalie, eight years later.

When Scott was four, his father bought him his first pair of hockey skates. Scott was a very active and very coordinated little boy, and as Carlos likes to say, "If you're going to live in Alaska, you've got to skate." By this time most of Scott's friends had already

Did You Know?

Scott's father never played hockey, but as a teenager he and his friends saw many games. The minor-league San Diego Gulls played near his house. "A big high-school date was to take your girl to a hockey game," Carlos remembers. One of the stars of the Gulls was veteran Willie O'Ree, who years earlier had been the first black player in the National Hockey League. Little did Carlos imagine that his own son would one day become the NHL's first Hispanic player!

started playing hockey and could move around the ice smoothly. Afraid to embarrass himself, Scott tried to convince his mother that hockey was a bad idea.

"I couldn't skate," he admits. "And I was afraid the other kids would make fun of me. I wanted to quit, I told my mom I was going to get hurt, that it was too rough. My mom told my dad I shouldn't play."

Carlos convinced Dalia that their son would be fine. He told her that, if she was afraid to see him injured, then she did not have to watch him play. Then he told Scott to go out and enjoy himself. Although the boy's skating technique was awkward (and some say it still is!) he managed to get where he needed to go, and he had terrific instincts. Encouraged by what he saw, Carlos took Scott to see some "real" hockey at the University of Alaska–Anchorage. Scott was very excited to see hockey played at full speed. The star of the Seawolves was a wing named Dan Larson. He became Scott's first sports hero.

Scott began watching hockey games on television. He copied the moves of the best players while playing in his living room. He would make up his own games, where he was the star of the hapless Hartford Whalers taking on the Stanley Cup champion

Edmonton Oilers. Scott imagined himself outwitting superstars Wayne Gretzky and Mark Messier. In doing so, he began to develop a deep under-standing of the little things it takes to be a successful hockey player.

This became clear as soon as Scott joined an organized team. He first played in a league sponsored by the Boys and Girls Club, then moved into Atom hockey and then Mite hockey. These are the beginning levels of youth hockey, where five-,

"I'd just spent $50 for a new pair of skates—no way am I going to let him quit the first day!"

CARLOS GOMEZ

Doug Gilmour,
the player Scott
admired most

six-, and seven-year-olds get their first real taste of the sport. Although smaller than a lot of the other kids, Scott seemed to have something special. A coach only had to show him something once, and soon it was part of his game.

At the age of eight, Scott joined the Mat-Su Alaska Eagles and became one of the team's best players. At 10, he moved up to the Anchorage North Stars, which took only the city's top young talent. By the age of 12, Scott was playing Midget hockey for the Alaska All-Stars, which is as high as a youth-level player can go in Alaska. By this time, he was totally hooked on hockey. Scott would rise before the sun most mornings and go to the nearby Tikishla skating rink to take advantage of the empty ice. There he would imagine himself playing in the NHL, like his hero, Doug Gilmour. Gilmour was an undersized center who skated fast, passed beautifully, and gave everything he had at both ends of the ice—just like Scott.

Scott could "see the ice" better than anyone on his team. He knew where every other player was, and what each was going to do next. It was as if he could see into the future. This made him an excellent passer, because he often knew when and where a teammate would be before that teammate did! It was amazing how he could put the puck right on a teammate's stick the moment he got open. Scott's good instincts also made him a dangerous scorer. As he prepared to shoot, he would glance up and "read" the goalie to determine where his weak spot was. Then he would fire a shot at that location. Very often it would sail into the net untouched.

Scott realized that the better he knew his teammates *off* the ice, the better he would play with them *on* the ice. So in addition to their practices, the All-Stars would gather at the Gomez house at 1812 Toklat Street for floor hockey games. Carlos and Dalia held their breath as the boys banged around the house, but they liked the fact that their son was so close to his friends. They were also pleased that Scott was getting along with children of other races—white, black, Hispanic, Asian, and Native American. "Where I come from," says Scott, "race didn't matter."

Hockey has been a way of life in the Gomez home since Scott received his first pair of skates. Here family and friends (left to right) watch an NHL game: uncle Juan, cousin Xiunell, friend Steve Agee, sister Natalie, cousin Erandy, mother Dalia, and father Carlos.

Junior Achiever

chapter 1

*"I've always had a good
eye to see who is open."*
— SCOTT GOMEZ

here have been only a few famous athletes from the state of Alaska. When Scott Gomez was a teenager, the most famous were Susan Butcher and Mark Schlereth. Butcher was a four-time winner of the Iditarod, a grueling dogsled race that covers 1,162 miles (1,870 km) of Alaskan wilderness. Schlereth, who grew up in Anchorage, was one of the National Football League's top offensive linemen. When Scott was 11, he watched Schlereth help the Washington Redskins win the Super Bowl.

When Scott entered East High School, he shared the campus with the

*Susan Butcher,
Alaska's most famous athlete*

Alaskans Mark Schlereth (left) and Trajan Langdon (right) gave Scott and other young athletes in Anchorage a couple of hometown heroes to cheer for.

greatest basketball player Alaska had ever produced. His name was Trajan Langdon, and he was a senior when Scott was a freshman. Langdon stood 6 feet 3 inches (191 cm) and had a sweet jumpshot. An excellent student, he was being recruited by several major colleges in the United States. He eventually accepted a scholarship from Duke University and went on to play in the NBA. Scott was in such awe of Langdon that he had to get a friend to ask him to sign his yearbook. It is still the centerpiece of Scott's memorabilia collection. "Trajan put Alaska on the map,"claims Scott.

By this time, Scott was drawing a lot of attention, too. Besides continuing to play for the Alaska All-Stars, he was the best player on the school team. During his sophomore year, he led the East High Thunderbirds to the state championship and

Did You Know?

Scott was a decent student in high school, although the early-morning practices made it hard to stay up late and study. His most embarrassing academic moment was when he received a D during his freshman year...in Spanish!

was honored as Player of the Year. He won this award again as a junior, when he tallied 101 points in just 27 games. A player gets a point for scoring a goal or assisting on one. That meant Scott played a role in nearly four goals per game! Scott also led the Alaska All-Stars to the national Midget championship. For the first time, hockey people in the United States were getting a look at him, and they liked what they saw.

When Scott turned 16, he became eligible to play in the United States Junior Hockey League. He was claimed by the Sioux City, Iowa, team. The USJHL offered a chance to play against the country's top teenagers. Scott had his sights set on playing pro hockey, and the Gomezes agreed that it was an important step toward becoming an NHL-caliber player. There was just one problem. Sioux City played in a small rink, and Scott's talents were better suited to a pro-size surface. The more room he had to skate, the greater the chance he had of making things happen—and the harder it would be for opponents to line him up and check him into the boards.

Scott's father voiced his concerns to Sioux City, and asked the team to trade Scott. When they refused, the Gomezes turned to the British Columbia Junior Hockey League in Canada. Scott agreed to play for the South Surrey Eagles. Although the quality of play was a notch below the USJHL, it was still very good. Brett Hull and Paul Kariya had played in this league and went on to become big stars in the NHL. When

Scott (11) chases down a rival skater from Lathrop High School during a 1994 tournament.

Scott (right) poke-checks the puck away from an enemy player during the 1995 state championship game. Defense like this made him a hot property in junior hockey.

Sioux City heard about the deal, they quickly traded Scott's rights to the Lincoln Stars, who played in a better facility. But it was too late. Although he had not signed anything, Scott declined to play for the Stars. He had given his word to the Eagles, and Carlos had always told him that a person's word should count for something.

The 1996–1997 season was Scott's first away from home. South Surrey is located near Vancouver, Canada, just over the border from the state of Washington. The Gomezes found a nice family to host their son, but he still missed home terribly. During the year, he spent $1,800 just calling home. "People don't realize how tough that was," he says. "I was only sixteen!"

Once Scott hit the ice, however, his worries melted away. Coach Rick Lanz placed him on the team's first line, between wings Shane Kuss and Rodney Bowers. Combining the initials from their last names, the teenagers became the "KGB Line" and proceeded to threaten several league scoring records. At season's end, the KGB Line

junior *stats*

SEASON	TEAM	GAMES	GOALS	ASSISTS	POINTS
1994–1995	East High T-Birds	28	30	48	78
1995–1996	East High T-Birds	27	56*	49	101*
	Anchorage	40	70*	67*	137*
1996–1997	South Surrey	56	48	76	124

* LED LEAGUE

junior *highlights*

BCJHL All-Rookie Team 1997
BCJHL All-Star 1997
BCJHL Champion 1997

accounted for 337 points. Scott finished second to Kuss in the BCJHL scoring race with 48 goals and 76 assists for 124 points, but was named the team's Most Valuable Player. Scott also was a league All-Star and Rookie of the Year. "That year was one of the finest times, the best experiences, I've ever had," says Scott. "Rick taught me so much about what it took to make it to the NHL."

Scott's game continued to grow during the postseason tournaments in which South Surrey competed. After winning the Cliff McNabb Memorial trophy as the top team in the BCJHL's Coastal Division, the Eagles went on to win the league championship. From there, South Surrey captured the Provincial Junior championship, then the Pacific Region championship, and finally the Western Canadian championship. Despite starting the year as a Tier II team, the Eagles made it all the way to the Canadian Junior A finals before falling to the Summerside team from Prince Edward Island. It was one of the greatest runs in the history of junior hockey.

Great Scotts!

The Alaska All-Stars had an impressive squad in the early 1990s. One of Scott's teammates was Scott Parker (left), who was the first pick of the Colorado Avalanche in the 1998 NHL Draft.

Devil of a Draft

chapter }

"I don't look at it like I'm breaking a barrier. I just want to be judged on how I play."

— SCOTT GOMEZ

Scott Gomez was now a major prospect. He also was becoming a "human interest" story. After his amazing year for South Surrey, hockey writers across Canada and the United States began predicting that he would one day break the NHL's "Latino Barrier." No such barrier ever existed, of course. It was just that no one with a Hispanic heritage had made it that far before. From Scott's point of view, he did not really like the extra attention. He wanted things to be like they were back in Anchorage. "I'm proud of my heritage," he says, "but growing up it wasn't: *There's Scott Gomez, the Mexican hockey player.* It was more like: *There's Scott Gomez, the hockey player.*"

Scott fakes out the goalie before scoring an easy goal.
His stick-handling improved as he advanced toward the NHL.

Scott took another step forward during the 1997–1998 season when he moved to Kennewick, Washington, and joined the Tri-City Americans of the Western Hockey League. The WHL has been around since the mid-1960s, and it has a reputation for taking promising youngsters and either shaping them up or burning them out. NHL scouts watched 17-year-old Scott with great interest, because he would be eligible for the pro draft once he turned 18. Would he light up the WHL, they wondered, or would he go down in flames?

Early in the year, the answer looked bad. Scott injured his shoulder and tried to play through the pain. It hurt when he checked, and it hurt when he shot, and it hurt when he battled for the puck along the boards. He wanted to play his normal game but he just could not. At mid-season, Scott joined Team USA at the World Junior

Did You Know?

Scott's Team USA roommate at the 1997 World Junior Championships was Mike York. Two years later they were battling for NHL Rookie of the Year honors!

Championships, and he was just a shadow of the player he had been a year before. After returning to the Tri-City Americans for the second half of the WHL season, Scott finally began to play pain-free and he finished strong. Although injuries limited him to just 45 games, Scott ended up with 12 goals and 37 assists for 49 points—not great, but not bad either.

As the NHL Draft approached, opinions on Scott were still mixed. Some projected him as a Top 10 pick. They liked his creativity and aggressiveness, and believed that his skills would carry him far in the pros. Others worried that Scott was just a shade too small to make it in the NHL. At 5 feet 11 inches (180 cm) and just under 200 pounds (91 kg), he would be one of the smaller players in the league. His critics claimed that the bad shoulder might never heal, or that it could be the first in a long line of injuries that would plague him throughout his career.

One team was positive, however, that Scott was worthy of a first-round pick: the New Jersey Devils. The Devils were a team that won with remarkable goaltending and a suffocating defense. In 1995 the Devils had captured the Stanley Cup. They had become NHL champs by waiting for opponents to make careless errors, and then converting those mistakes into goals. The 1995 club featured a handful of special players— players who had the good fundamentals to play defense, but also the offensive spark to

General Manager Lou Lamoriello (left) and John McMullen, who owned the Devils in 1998, believed that drafting Scott was a major step in their quest to recapture the Stanley Cup.

put the puck in the net. In the years following their title, the Devils had fallen short of the Stanley Cup because they did not have enough of these players. Scott Gomez, they believed, was this type of player.

Where other teams saw a little man who could be bulldozed by burly defensemen, General Manager Lou Lamoriello saw a strong skater who was tough to knock down on the open ice. Where others feared that Scott would be crushed by larger opponents behind the net, Lamoriello and his staff saw

Did You Know?

In all, nine centers were taken before Scott in the 1998 NHL Draft, including Nikolai Antropov, Alex Tanguay, Eric Chouinard, Simon Gagne, and Milan Kraft. It will be interesting to see how many of these first-rounders are still around a few years from now.

someone who used the net to shield himself when he had the puck, and who was most dangerous when he was *not* in front of the goal. The greatest player in history, Wayne Gretzky, possessed these very same skills.

The Devils picked 26th in the draft. They watched anxiously as one name after another came off the board. Center Vincent Lecavalier went first, to the Tampa Bay Lightning. David Legwand, another center, was selected with the next pick, by the Nashville Predators. Two more centers, Rico Fata and Manny Malhotra, were taken with picks six and seven. In New Jersey's eyes, Scott was as good as any of the remaining centers, so they held out little hope he would be available. But when the Devils' pick finally came around, *both* of the players they wanted—Scott Gomez and defenseman Mike Van Ryn—were still available! The Devils grabbed Van Ryn, then traded two second-round picks to the Dallas Stars, who owned the next choice. With the Stars' pick, Lamoriello selected Scott.

Scott was both pleased and disappointed. He felt at home with the Devils. In fact, he had met Lamoriello in New Jersey while touring with the U.S. junior team the previous winter, and they had gotten along well. When the GM was not looking, Scott wrote his name on the bottom of the Devils' depth chart (a list of every player in the organization from best to worst), then asked Lamoriello how he could have slipped so far. "He looked at the board and saw what I had done and just laughed," remembers Scott.

He was unhappy, however, about dropping so low in the draft. Scott had flown his entire family down from Anchorage to watch his name get called in the first round. When the Devils took Van Ryn, his heart sank because the Dallas Stars had the final choice in the first round. As the crowd awaited Dallas' pick, David Conte, New Jersey's Director of Scouting, caught Scott's eye and gave him a wink. Scott had no idea what was happening. When he heard his name announced moments later, he figured it all out. He was a first-rounder after all.

"I didn't want to like him because he was just another little guy. But the more I watched, the more I liked him. I was sold. He's a great playmaker—a top-notch player."
ALL-TIME GREAT GERRY CHEEVERS

Breaking
the Ice

chapter 4

"Juniors was fun...
here, it's all business."
— SCOTT GOMEZ

hortly after the draft, the New Jersey Devils invited Scott Gomez to training camp. Although the team had already decided to farm him out to the
minor leagues, they wanted him to get a taste of the big time so he would
have something to work hard for.
Scott was very polite. He called
everyone by their last name—Mr.
Stevens, Mr. Brodeur, Mr. Holik.

"He's got great skills and he
brings players around him to a
higher level. There is always
room for a player like that."
TEAMMATE MARTIN BRODEUR

Scott was "Mr. Polite" during his first training camp with the Devils.
His teammates thought he was pretty funny—until
they saw how seriously he played.

Taskmaster Vladimir Bure whipped Scott into shape for his first NHL season.

They thought he was funny, but once they saw him play the Devils knew he was seriously good. No one doubted that he would be playing with them by the year 2000.

In the meantime, Scott had something to prove back in the Western Hockey League, where the Devils sent him after camp. Now 100 percent healthy, he took the WHL by storm. Opponents who remembered him from the previous season were caught completely off-guard, as Scott scored 30 goals and collected 78 assists in just 58 games. He also played for the U.S. junior team again, this time with more power and confidence. He collected 3 goals and 7 assists in 7 tournament games.

The Devils were thrilled with Scott's progress, but were concerned that he was not in good enough shape to take the next step in his career. There is a big difference between doing well in the WHL and playing 80-plus games in the NHL. The team invited Scott to New Jersey over the summer to train with Vladimir Bure. A former Russian Olympian, Bure knew how to get hockey players into shape. His sons Pavel and Valeri were already NHL stars. Pavel, in fact, was considered one of the five best players in the game.

Scott rented an apartment a few minutes from the Continental Arena and began his workouts. He was psyched to have a super summer. What started as an adventure, however, quickly turned into a daily torture routine. Bure pushed Scott to the limit, until Scott himself wondered whether he could make it. "It was the toughest thing I've ever been through," he says. "I wouldn't wish it on my worst enemy."

minor-league *stats*

SEASON	TEAM	GAMES	GOALS	ASSISTS	POINTS
1997–1998	Tri-City	45	12	37	49
1998–1999	Tri-City	58	30	78*	108

* LED LEAGUE

minor-league *highlights*

WHL First-Team All-Star 1999

When training camp opened, Scott was in the best shape of his life. Although nothing was promised to him, he felt from the first day that he would make the Devils. The Devils had other plans. The New Jersey organization has a history of bringing its young players along slowly, and wanted to send Scott back to the WHL for one more season. "I went in thinking, *I'm gonna make them keep me*," he says. "I just had a feeling I was going to make the team."

Coach Robbie Ftorek was impressed with Scott. He saw more quickness and more strength. He also saw the pinpoint passing and remarkable anticipation he had read about in the scouting reports. Clearly, the 19-year-old had the skills and maturity to survive in the NHL. Then again, Ftorek had nothing to lose by sending him back to the minors.

Scott was in luck. Three key players were having contract disputes with the team—Patrik Elias, Brendan Morrison, and Petr Sykora. In their absence, Scott got a lot of ice time. The more he played (and the more irritated the Devils became with their holdouts) the more

After working with Vladimir Bure, Scott began to appreciate what Pavel had to go through to earn the stats on the back of his hockey card.

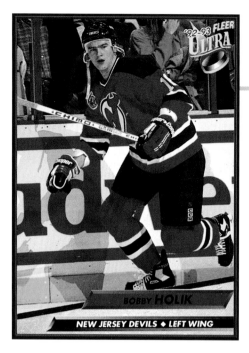

Scott was just 13 when this Bobby Holik card was issued. Six years later they were teammates!

Lamoriello and Ftorek thought about keeping Scott. They began playing him in specialty situations—on power plays and when the team was shorthanded—and saw that he had a good understanding of the game. They also recognized a quality that is unusual in a first-year player: His teammates seemed to play better when he was on the ice.

When Scott reported to camp, he was assigned number 48. High numbers like this usually go to players who are not expected to be around very long. With a few days to go before the final cut, assistant coach Larry Robinson tossed a new jersey at Scott. "You're number 23 now," he said. Scott knew instantly he had made the team!

What he did *not* know was how the Devils would do in 1999–2000. Nor did anyone else. New Jersey always put an excellent team on the ice, but come playoff time the Devils seemed to "find" a way to lose. Lamoriello decided it was time to shake things up and get rid of some older forwards. In their place, the team inserted a group of up-and-coming players. Scott and fellow rookie John Madden were part of this new wave, as were Sykora, Morrison, and Elias—all of whom had come to terms with the Devils early in the season. The hope was that these five players would blend with the more established forwards, including Bobby Holik, Jason Arnott, Brian Rolston, Sergei Nemchinov, and Randy McKay. New Jersey's defense was still rock-solid. Playing in front of goalie Martin Brodeur were Ken Daneyko, Lyle Odelein, Sheldon Souray, Brian Rafalski, speedy Scott Niedermayer, and superstar Scott Stevens.

Coach Robbie Ftorek was under a lot of pressure to get the Devils deep into the playoffs. The previous season, he had been outcoached in big games, and the players sometimes lacked confidence in his decisions. That is why the team hired Robinson as an assistant. A Hall-of-Fame defenseman with the legendary Montreal Canadiens in the

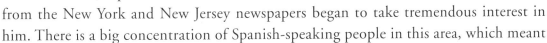

Coach Robbie Ftorek had much in common with Scott. In the 1970s he was one of the game's top "small" centers, once scoring 59 goals in a season.

1970s, he was the NHL's most respected back-liner. No one questioned Robinson on hockey matters—if Ftorek had his confidence, then surely the players would be confident, too.

As soon as Scott made the team, reporters from the New York and New Jersey newspapers began to take tremendous interest in him. There is a big concentration of Spanish-speaking people in this area, which meant that Scott's story might sell a lot of extra papers. Indeed, a lot of Latino sports fans who had never watched a hockey game started following the Devils. The NHL itself also jumped on the Scott Gomez bandwagon. The league was anxious to find new ways to promote itself, especially with the retirement of Wayne Gretzky following the 1998–1999 season. Scott was a great story.

He was used to this kind of attention, of course. Scott knew how to

"He's got the easygoing personality where nothing seems to bother him."
TEAMMATE SCOTT STEVENS

Welcome to the NHL, kid! Scott gets a chestful of pipe courtesy of Rich Pilon in a game against the Islanders.

answer just about every "race" question, and he also knew that if he played well enough, he would be thought of as a hockey star first and a Latino second. Still, he was amazed at how intensely New York–area interviewers focused on his background. "Sometimes they make it sound like I crossed the border two years ago with a bottle of tequila and a pair of skates," he laughs. "And *voilà*, I'm an NHLer!"

Occasionally, people would go a bit overboard. Like the reporter who dubbed him "hockey's Jackie Robinson." Robinson broke organized baseball's ban against African-Americans more than 50 years ago, and had to listen to endless insults from racist fans. "People bring up Jackie Robinson and try to compare me to him and it isn't even close," says Scott.

The Face of
Hockey

Of the four major team sports in North America, hockey has the least "ethnic diversity." About half the players in Major League Baseball, for example, are either black, Hispanic, or Asian. In the National Hockey League, more than 95 percent (19 in 20) of the players are white. Scott says that he faced many more people of color in junior hockey—including numerous Native Americans—and believes that soon the NHL will see a lot of diversity. Willie O'Ree (right), who became the NHL's first black player in 1958, agrees. "Eventually, we'll see more people of color in the league," predicts O'Ree, who now works for the NHL.

Remarkable Rookie

"I really feel like part of the team."
— SCOTT GOMEZ

I t took Scott Gomez exactly two NHL games to make headlines for a reason other than his Latino heritage. In a game against the Ottawa Senators, he set up two goals with sweet passes. A few days later, he netted his first NHL goal against the New York Islanders, and added two more assists. After the game, goalie Felix Potvin told reporters that Scott had good "puck sense"—he knew exactly when to slip in front of the net and when to feed his teammates.

Scott proved to be a quick learner, too. Prior to each game, the coaches reviewed their opponents' tendencies. Time and again they saw him

"Scott is a playmaker, we all know that. That's why he was drafted."
TEAMMATE BOBBY HOLIK

Scott leaves a trail of Rangers behind as he zeroes in on the net. In New Jersey's December 26th game against the Rangers, he became the youngest Devil to score a "hat trick."

use this information to his advantage that very night. In his second meeting with the Senators, he scored the winning goal in a tight game when he fired a wrist shot past the stick of Ron Tugnutt. Robbie Ftorek and Larry Robinson were beaming when Scott skated back to the bench. A couple of hours earlier, they had warned him that Tugnutt had one of the quickest gloves in the business, and he had remembered to shoot to the goalie's slower stick side. Counting an assist he got earlier in the contest, Scott now had 21 points in his first 19 NHL games—tops on the team. Not bad for a teenager who was ticketed for the WHL a couple of months earlier!

The biggest contribution Scott made to the Devils could not be found in the statistics. He was having such a good time that he reminded the older players how much fun it was to play hockey. A year earlier, the Devils locker room was a tense and angry place. In 1999–2000 everyone was smiling and joking. "I wondered what these guys were really like," Scott admits. Now he knows. Hockey players may look tough, he says, "but they are kids at heart—it's a business, but the reason we all start playing is it's fun."

Making the cover of **THE HOCKEY NEWS** *was one of the biggest thrills of Scott's career.*

Three days after Scott turned 20, the Devils went across the Hudson River to play the New York Rangers. With his parents and younger sister Natalie in the stands, Scott scored all three goals in a 3–3 tie. He became the youngest Devil ever to get a "hat trick."

Scott may have been young, but more and more, he was handling himself like an old-timer. When rookies start enjoying some success in the NHL, opponents usually try to intimidate them. But when they tried rough tactics with Scott, he kept his cool and took advantage of their aggressive play. If two defenders converged on him, he knew a teammate had to be open somewhere—and usually found a way to slide the puck to him. When other teams saw how well the rookie could pass under pressure, they laid off and gave him the respect he deserved.

In January, Scott was leading all first-year NHL players in points. His season was almost cut short, however, when teammate Sheldon Souray smacked him in the chin with a stick in practice. Scott's tongue was sticking out at the time, and he almost bit it off. He went to the hospital and got it stitched

Did You Know?

During his fabulous rookie year, Scott's teammates decided to say thank you by setting up a dinner with his hero, Doug Gilmour. "Gomer," as the Devils called Scott, was so surprised he could hardly speak during the meal. Now he is afraid that "Gilmour thinks I'm an idiot."

back together, but he could not talk for several days. His teammates thought it was hilarious (hockey players have a strange sense of humor) and from then on his nickname was "Mumbles."

Scott literally *was* speechless when, a few days later, Lou Lamoriello summoned him to his office. Scott was terrified. He thought he had broken a team rule. The General Manager sat him down and told the nervous 20-year-old that he had been selected to play in the NHL All-Star Game. *No way!* Scott was sure he was the target of an elaborate prank. It took a while before he could believe it. Only two other rookies in team history had been All-Stars.

That February, Scott went to Toronto as a member of the North American All-Star squad. To see so many great players in one place was fantastic. He practically lost his mind when Mark Messier plunked down next to him in the locker room and started talking to him—and then Wayne Gretzky came by to say hello. It was like he was back in his living room playing floor hockey, only these guys were real!

After the All-Star Game, Scott picked up right where he'd left off. He was now playing left wing, with Brendan Morrison on right wing and veteran Claude Lemieux

Scott ducks under a check and looks for an open teammate. His ability to occupy two defenders at once has helped him become one of the league's top assist-getters.

Sometimes they just don't go in. Scott watches as Atlanta's Damian Rhodes robs him of an easy goal.

centering. Lemieux, acquired earlier in the year, was a bona fide NHL legend. In 1995, Lemieux carried the Devils to several victories on their way to the Stanley Cup, and was awarded the Conn Smyth Trophy as the NHL's postseason MVP. Lemieux had also won Stanley Cups with the Montreal Canadiens and Colorado Rockies, and in 1997 had led all players in postseason goals in a losing cause. No one played better in big games.

This new line clicked for the Devils. The two young wings felt like Lemieux was a second coach on the ice, and as a result they became much more consistent players. Lemieux was shocked when he heard how young Scott was. He had never seen such a mature young player.

Every March in the NHL, teams that believe they can win the Stanley Cup try to make trades to improve themselves for the playoffs. The Devils were no exception. Although they were in first place, Lou Lamoriello was not happy with the chemistry of the club. The players rarely seemed to be skating at full speed, and the energy that was there earlier in the season had started to fade away. Lamoriello could not look at any one player and say, "He's the problem." So he began to look at the coach. Robbie Ftorek was not motivating his players. In a stunning move, Lamoriello fired Ftorek with just eight games left in the season, and promoted Larry Robinson.

Scott was blown away. He began to see that the NHL postseason was serious business. Fun is fun, but when the playoffs roll around, nobody's job is safe.

Picking Up the Pace

chapter 6

"There's no way I didn't want to be a part of this."
— SCOTT GOMEZ

arry Robinson did his best to whip the Devils into shape in the time that remained, but the team won just half of its final eight games. This allowed the Philadelphia Flyers to slip past New Jersey and into first place. Scott and his teammates played well some nights, and not so well other nights. Late in the season, the Devils traded Brendan Morrison for veteran wing Alexander Mogilny. Coach Robinson shifted slick-passing Scott back to center between Mogilny and Claude Lemieux. He was gambling that another position switch would not rattle Scott. Sometimes a rookie can become confused if he has to play too many positions in the same season. It was no problem for Scott. "I don't mind moving," he insists.

It took a few weeks, but Larry Robinson finally got the Devils playing excellent hockey.

Scott is thwarted by Panthers veteran Mike Vernon in the playoffs. Scott was amazed how much faster the game was played during the postseason.

"Whatever it takes to make the team successful."

This gave the Devils a superb new line for the playoffs. Mogilny was the sharpshooter, Scott the playmaker, and Lemieux the "enforcer." The Devils matched this talented line against an opponent's number-three line, which gave New Jersey a big advantage. They pressed this advantage in the first game of their opening-round series with the Florida Panthers. With the score 3–2 and Florida looking to tie things up, Scott knocked in the game-winning goal in a 4–3 victory. Scott Stevens scored the winning goal in the next game, to give the Devils a 2 games to 0 lead in the best-of-seven series. Game Three was a close one, too, but Brian Rafalski scored on a wrist shot to give New Jersey a 2–1 win. Finally, in Game Four, the Devils got an easy victory, as Patrik Elias, Rob Niedermayer, and Sergei Nemchinov starred in a 4–1 win to nail down a series sweep.

New Jersey's second-round opponent was the Toronto Maple Leafs. The Leafs had two big stars, center Mats Sundin and goalie Curtis Joseph. Joseph and Martin Brodeur put on a

Did You Know?

Florida's top player during the 2000 playoffs was Pavel Bure, the son of the man who got Scott in shape for his rookie season.

goaltending clinic in the first two games, with each making several spectacular saves. Toronto won the first game, 2–1, and the Devils took the next one, 1–0. Scott saw little ice time in these games. Coach Robinson felt that he had been a step slow in the

Florida series, and chose not to play him very much against the Maple Leafs. Scott and his coach had a talk. Scott insisted that he was playing the game at the same pace he always did. Robinson agreed. The difference was that everyone *else* had put their game into high gear, but Scott had not. This is playoff time, Robinson explained. Either you dig down and find that extra energy, or you sit.

Scott got the message. "If that doesn't light a fire under you, I don't know what does," he says. "I guess I was kind of taking things for granted, maybe thinking I had a good year, that I deserved this or that. It doesn't work that way."

Coach Robinson gave Scott one more chance. Fifteen minutes into the first period of Game Three, the rookie was on the ice when he spotted a loose puck dribbling at the top of the right circle. Scott made up his mind to get it first, and he did. Then he swooped into the slot and flicked a wrist shot past Joseph to give the Devils a 2–0 advantage. New Jersey won the game to take a 2–1 series lead. The Leafs tied it up in Game Four, but Scott played well again and scored another goal. Game Five promised to be the pivotal contest. Whoever won this game would go up 3–2 and need just one more victory to advance to the Eastern Conference finals.

Cheered wildly by their home crowd, Toronto came out flying. Late in the second period, they were ahead 2–1 and looking to blow the game wide open. But the Devils tied the score when Scott shoveled a pass to Nemchinov, who found the back of the net. In the third period, Scott stickhandled his way into Maple Leaf territory

Scott gets howls of encouragement from new linemates Alexander Mogilny (89) and Claude Lemieux after scoring against the Maple Leafs.

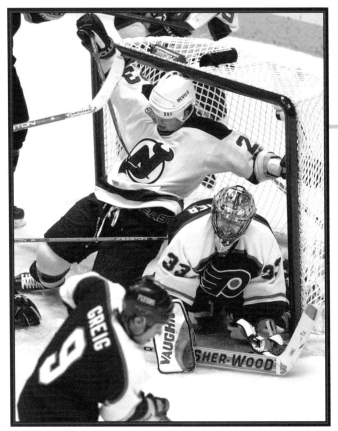

Scott winces as his head hits the goal during Game Four of New Jersey's playoff series with the Flyers. He winced again after the game, when Coach Robinson ripped into the team for their poor play.

and waited patiently for the Toronto defense to come to him. When they did he executed a nifty behind-the-back drop pass to Vladimir Malakhov, who blasted a slap shot past Joseph. The Devils held on for a 4–3 win. Back in New Jersey, the Devils closed out the series with a 3–0 victory. In the loser's locker room, Joseph said that Scott's play in the last four games made the difference.

The New Jersey Devils were now just one step away from the Stanley Cup Finals. The team they needed to beat was the Philadelphia Flyers. The Flyers were a big, tough squad that had come together after losing their best player, Eric Lindros, to a severe concussion. The Flyers were mean and talented. And they had a couple of young playoff stars in goalie Brian Boucher and defenseman Andy Delmore. They were looking like a team on a mission. But in Game One, it was the Devils that came out strong. They scored three times in the opening period, and added a fourth goal late in the game when Scott set up Lemieux with a nice pass. Brodeur made every save but one in a 4–1 win. The Flyers came right back and played great hockey in Game Two. Despite a goal and assist from Scott, the Devils could not stop Philadelphia, which won 4–3 to knot the series.

The teams moved to New Jersey for the next two games. Devils fans were hoping for two wins on their home ice, but instead they got two losses. The Flyers won 4–2 and 3–1, outshooting, outchecking, and outhustling the Devils time after time. In the third period of Game Four, Coach Robinson lost his cool and began screaming at his players right in front of the fans. In the locker room after the game, his tirade continued. *Where is your heart? Where is your pride?* Robinson kicked a trash can across the room. The players were amazed. They had known Robinson to be a quiet, reserved man who never showed his feelings.

The Devils were in a tough spot. Not since the days when the NHL was a tiny six-team league had a team come back from 3–1 this late in the playoffs. The players agreed to take things one game at a time, play their hearts out, and rewrite the history books. Inspired by their coach, they won Game Five, 4–1. Game Six was a classic, with neither team scoring until late in the final period. Scott's line came through twice, with goals by Lemieux and Mogilny, to escape with a 2–1 victory.

Game Seven, in Philadelphia, was one for the books. The Flyers fans cheered the return of their hero, Lindros, who had defied doctors' orders and rejoined the team. It

was Lindros, in fact, who netted Philadelphia's lone goal in Game Six. Eight minutes into this game, however, Stevens crashed into Lindros and sent him sprawling. The big center had to be helped off the ice, and he did not return. Fifty-two more minutes of tense, hard-hitting action followed. With the teams tied 1–1, Elias scored the game-winning goal and the spectacular Brodeur made the slim lead stand up. The Devils had beaten history and the Flyers to advance to the finals.

Scott gets run down by Kent Manderville in Game Seven of the Flyers series. The Devils won 2–1 to advance to the Stanley Cup finals.

Capturing the Cup

chapter 7

"I was there from day one to the end. I never got sent down."

— SCOTT GOMEZ

The 2000 Stanley Cup Finals promised to be an interesting series. The Devils were playing the Dallas Stars, who had won the Cup the year before. The Stars were just that—a collection of big-name players known to all hockey fans. Their leader was center Mike Modano, a thrilling scorer. On right wing was hard-shooting Brett Hull, who had scored his 600th career goal earlier in the year. The team's power play starred Joe Nieuwendyk, the defense was held together by monstrous Derian Hatcher, and in goal was the acrobatic Ed Belfour.

"He's a heck of a hockey player."

TEAMMATE BOBBY HOLIK

Mike Modano of the Dallas Stars loses this battle with Martin Brodeur. The defending champs were upended by New Jersey's great goaltending and timely scoring.

The Devils did not match up well man-to-man, so they were considered big under-dogs. But Coach Robinson believed that, as a team, his players were every bit as good as the Stars. The key to the series for New Jersey would be its defense and goaltending. If the Devils could shut down the Dallas attack, its forwards would get enough good chances to beat Belfour.

This plan worked to perfection in Game One. Although the Stars did manage to score three goals, the Devils scored seven. Belfour was so rattled that he had to leave the game in the third period. The veteran returned to the nets in Game Two and played marvelously, as Dallas tied the series with a 2–1 win. New Jersey's only goal came when Scott drew three defenders to him and then kicked a pass forward to Alexander Mogilny, who wristed it home.

The finals moved to Dallas, where the Stars owned an impressive 9–1 record in the playoffs. Three periods later their record was 9–2. Jason Arnott and Petr Sykora scored for the Devils, and Martin Brodeur made a breathtaking save on Modano with 49 seconds left to preserve a 2–1 win. Brodeur was fabulous again in Game Four. After allowing Nieuwendyk to score in the second period, he shut Dallas down the rest of the way. The

Did You Know?

Scott was the only Devil to appear in every single one of the team's games in 1999-2000.

Devils won 2–1 again, on third-period goals by John Madden and Brian Rafalski.

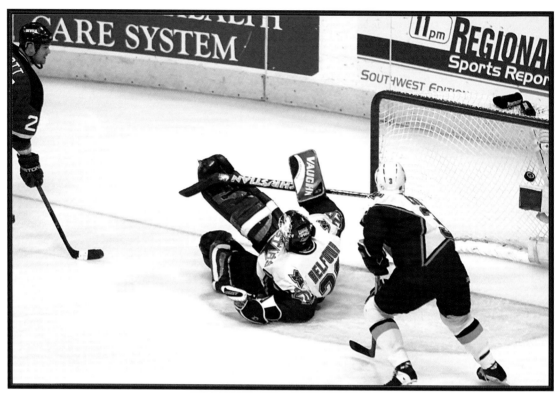

Ed Belfour goes low, but the puck goes high as Jason Arnott (left) watches the goal that delivered the Stanley Cup to New Jersey.

Game Five, back in New Jersey, featured perhaps the finest playoff goaltending anyone had ever seen. Through three periods and two overtimes, Brodeur and Belfour made one miraculous save after another in an action-packed 0–0 game. Six minutes into the third overtime, Modano swooped in on Brodeur and tipped a shot by Hull that found its way into the net. It was a great play that ended the longest scoreless tie in postseason history.

The Devils had made it to the finals by overcoming a 3–1 deficit. They were not about to let the Stars do the same to them. In Game Six, everyone on the team played all out, all night. Once again, the game went into overtime. But this time it was New Jersey that broke through. In the second extra period, Jason Arnott flicked a shot past Belfour to give the Devils the Stanley Cup. Veteran Scott Stevens, who quieted the Dallas offense all series long, won the Conn Smyth Trophy as MVP. But the difference in this hard-fought series was the play of New Jersey's young guns, the guys Lou

Scott takes the Stanley Cup from MVP Scott Stevens during the team's victory celebration.

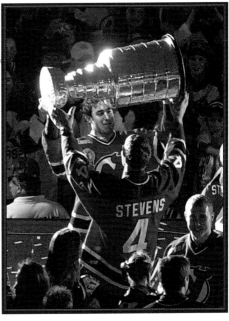

Lamoriello had brought in at the beginning of the season. Six of the team's sixteen game-deciding goals were scored by rookies.

Scott won more than the Stanley Cup in his rookie year. After the playoffs, he was selected by his fellow players as hockey's top first-year performer. He also won the Calder Memorial Trophy as the NHL's Rookie of the Year. Besides leading all rookies with 70 points, Scott finished eighth in the league overall with 51 assists.

That summer, each member of the Devils got to keep the Stanley Cup for a few days. When it was Scott's turn, he took it back home to Anchorage, where 500 fans greeted him at the airport. His first two stops were a retirement home and a hospital, where he signed autographs and let fans see the Stanley Cup up close. Then Scott and the trophy were transported by dogsled to downtown Anchorage, where 8,000 people cheered him. Scott was then honored with a traditional Native American blanket toss. A group of Alaskan elders threw him 20 feet (6 meters) in the air on a gigantic sealskin blanket. At the end of the day, he set the Stanley Cup out on the front lawn and let his neighbors admire it. "This is yours," he told them. "Kiss it, grab it, do whatever."

NHL *stats*

SEASON	TEAM	GAMES	GOALS	ASSISTS	POINTS
1999–2000	New Jersey	82	19	51	70

NHL *highlights*

NHL All-Star 2000
Calder Cup Winner (Rookie of the Year) 2000
Stanley Cup Champion 2000

Scott hoists the Stanley Cup for the people of Anchorage, as they prepare to honor him with a Native American blanket toss.

Something to Smile About

"There's no question he loves the game...he puts everything aside and just plays and has fun."

— TEAMMATE SCOTT STEVENS

Scott Gomez returned to camp to prepare for the 2000–2001 season. Larry Robinson told Scott he was counting on him taking another step forward during his second year. He already was the team's best passer and playmaker, but the coach also thought Scott could be a consistent 30-goal scorer. The extra pressure showed when the season began. Over the first month, Scott seemed less relaxed. There were fewer *Cools* and *Awesomes*, and also fewer goals and assists. And when he did get a scoring chance, he sometimes tried to make too difficult a play—and ended up with nothing.

As the NHL's first Hispanic player, Scott has attracted thousands of new fans to hockey memorabilia collecting. His card is usually the first they buy.

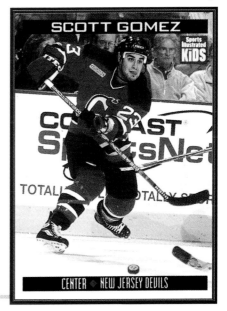

Scott has found that opponents give him a lot less open ice these days. No problem—he is used to creating his own.

With help from Bobby Holik and Randy McKay, Scott finally came out of his slump. McKay kept telling him to be himself, to relax. Holik said a player's second season is often his hardest, but assured him that his points would come. Coach Robinson told Scott that he was no longer an "unknown." As New Jersey's top assist man, opponents were giving him a lot less room to operate. It was his job to open up the ice—to make those opponents back off by continuing to raise his level of play. Scott did just that. He stopped trying to make every pass perfect, and just passed. He stopped attempting to shoot the puck through razor-thin openings and just shot the puck. Scott let his talent take over, and soon he was back to his old self again.

The Scott Gomez the league had to deal with in 2000–2001 was a year smarter and a year stronger. He was better on defense and face-offs, and murder on the open ice. Those who wondered whether he was tough enough to stand up to the NHL's bullies got their answer. Anyone who tried to intimidate Scott could expect a vicious check or a well-placed chop of the stick in retaliation. He refused to back down. At the tender age of 21, he was playing like a tough old veteran.

Where does Scott go from here? He is the first to admit there is room for improvement. To be the big-time goal scorer the team wants him to be, he must become a better "finisher" around the net. That means being able to put back loose rebounds quickly and accurately, and it also means developing one-on-one moves that will work against bigger players. As for the mental side of Scott's game, well, most experts agree that he is already the brightest young player in the league.

Another thing everyone agrees on is that Scott's attitude could not be any better. He loves being a hockey player, and sometimes he cannot believe how far he has come. "At the end of the day, when I am driving to the rink, it is still kind of, *'Wow! Holy cow! I'm in the NHL!'*" Scott admits. "I still get chills thinking about it."

Sometimes he just has to shake his head in wonder. "This life I'm living, it's amazing."

No matter where hockey takes Scott, his heart will always be back in Alaska. He returns after each season to visit his family and work with the kids of Anchorage.

Index